# FAILURE HAS NO ALIBI

## Learning from the Lessons that Failure Teaches

**DR. CHERYL A. LENTZ**

Foreword by Jim Stovall
Best-selling author of *The Ultimate Gift*

*Failure Has No Alibi:*
*Learning From the Lessons Failure Teaches*

**Pensiero Press** • http://www.PensieroPress.com

https://Twitter.com/DrCherylLentz
https://www.Facebook.com/Dr.Cheryl.Lentz
https://www.Linkedin.com/in/drcheryllentz/
https://www.Youtube.com/drcheryllentz
https://www.Instagram.com/drcheryllentz/
Email: drcheryllentz@gmail.com

All rights reserved. No part of this book may be reproduced or transmitted in any form or by any means, graphic, electronic, or mechanical, including photocopying, recording, taping, Web distribution, or by any informational storage and retrieval system without written permission from the publisher except for the inclusion of brief quotations in a review or scholarly reference.

Books are available through Pensiero Press at special discounts for bulk purchases for the purpose of sales promotion, seminar attendance, or educational purposes.

Copyright © 2020 by Pensiero Press

ISBN: 978-1-7356817-5-7

*Cover design and interior by Gary Rosenberg

Printed in the United States of America

10  9  8  7  6  5  4  3  2  1

# CONTENTS

Testimonials   v

Acknowledgments   xi

Foreword   xiii

Preface   xvii

**CHAPTER 1**
The First F   1

**CHAPTER 2**
The Day the Music Died   7

**CHAPTER 3**
Failure Came in Waves   13

**CHAPTER 4**
Part Deux: Lost Love   19

**CHAPTER 5**
Failure is a Gift   29

**CHAPTER 6**
Turn Into the Wave   33

### CHAPTER 7
Choose to Dance   37

### CHAPTER 8
Ask the Right Questions   43

### CHAPTER 9
What is Your Legacy?   47

### CHAPTER 10
Speak From the Heart   51

### CHAPTER 11
No Regrets   55

About the Author   59

# TESTIMONIALS

Success requires accountability, belief in yourself, and the ability to keep showing up one more time than you got knocked down. Remember, your greatest success just might be Three Feet From Gold.

**Dr. Greg Reid**

www.GregReid.com

Problems are nothing more than challenges. And there is a gift behind every challenge including an opportunity. Problems are nothing more than frustrations, that's why they must be considered simple challenges. Identify the given with each challenge and the goal you are seeking. Keep it simple. Do not get lost in the journey along the way. Do not be afraid to fail. Making mistakes is part of your education and success. If you painted it the wrong color the first time, paint it a new color.

**Ron Klein**
*Grandfather of Possibilities*
thegrandfatherofpossibilities.com

Your heart will be touched as Dr. Cheryl shares her life's journey and powerful discovery around failure . . . that the key to succeeding sooner is to fail faster! You will be empowered through her transparent sharing of own life's challenges and the be inspired by her self-reflection, reinvention, and transformational message of hope. The strength of this book lies in its message that you can continue moving forward and find the gifts that failure can bring by teaching us inner wisdom to find our purpose along our own path. May you lean in and be willing to bring your gifts forward faster too.

**Rebecca Hall Gruyter**
Founder/Owner, Your Purpose Driven Practice
www.YourPurposeDrivePractice.com

Learning does not always happen in a formal classroom; sometimes one learns from the school of hard knocks and experience. No one benefits from playing small, particularly with one's personal passion. Dr.Cheryl recognizes the powerful gifts of failure from life's sometimes brutal moments, sharing with us some of her most epic failures that empowered her to

# TESTIMONIALS

move forward. She dares to be authentic and raw, offering us a glimpse along those difficult journeys. A must read to inspire you on your journey.

**Clarissa Burt**
CEO/Founder of *In the Limelight*
https://clarissaburt.com/
https://clarissaburt.com/magazine/

Having known Dr. Cheryl for 8 years now, the woman I met then could not have written this book. *Failure Has No Alibi* is a raw account of her transformation in discovering the direct route out of her head (the academic that she is) and into her heart (the now evolved woman that she has become.) This book is a perfect read for those struggling to get there as it teaches hope, determination, and success in falling in love with and believing in yourself.

**Elizabeth Phinney**
Healthy and Energetic Aging Expert
www.theagingcoach.com

This is a wonderful guide to take you through the journey of accepting yourself and your life path. Everything happens for a reason! Have gratitude and understanding for all of it along the way. It's an adventure.

### Crystal Rose

Spirit Guide, Psychic, and Love Coach
www.comfysoul.com

This is a wonderful guide to take you through the journey of accepting yourself and your life path. Everything happens for a reason! Have gratitude and understanding for all of it along the way. It's an adventure.

*"Success requires no explanations.
Failure permits no alibis."*

—Napoleon Hill

# ACKNOWLEDGMENTS

One does not go through life alone. Thank you to my Secret Knock (SK) Family, particularly my coach Dr. Greg Reid and Shannon Parsons. Since I joined the tribe many years ago, I have found kindred spirits in pursuit of this thing we call life. I am forever grateful for your welcome to the family, your continued love and support, and your gift of friendship, introduction, and connection to the many family members I continue to meet.

Thank you to Jim Stovall for joining this journey in writing the Foreword. Because of the connection to Napoleon Hill, what a perfect member of the SK family to write such an invitation.

Thank you to my team at Pensiero Press to include Gary Rosenberg for his brilliant cover design.

To Dr. Hamilton and the two greatest loves of my life, thank you for the greatest gifts of failure. Thank you for being my teachers and for helping me learn some of life's most painful yet important lessons. I may not have learned the lesson at the time, but I eventually got there, sometimes way too late, I know. I am sorry. I remain forever in your debt as a willing student and a work in progress.

# FOREWORD

Within the pages of this book, you are going to take a journey with my colleague Cheryl Lentz. You are going to learn a lot about Cheryl, her life, and what her experiences have taught her. But this is not a book about Cheryl. It is a book about you and me. Cheryl has just been kind enough to allow us to look into the reflection of her soul so we can examine ourselves. I believe, as it has been said, that an unexamined life is not worth living.

Here in the 21st century, we have more information and less reality than any generation of people that has ever lived. Social media forces us to look at everyone's "highlight reel" as they post the high points of their personal, family, and professional life. When we examine their highpoints and consider our own shortcomings, we are immediately confronted with this false reality of failure. Failure is nothing more than a preamble to success. It is the fertilizer for future growth and development.

As he was developing the lightbulb, Thomas Edison failed hundreds of times in finding the proper filament to turn darkness into light for the whole world. He never considered any of these experiments a failure. He simply looked upon them as successfully discovering another filament that would not work. Failure is a great indicator of future success.

As a blind person myself, I am a huge fan of sports that are broadcast on the radio. Thanks to the wonderful technology that allows satellite radio to exist, throughout the spring, summer, and fall, you will inevitably find me listening to a ball game as a part of my daily routine. As a fan and student of baseball and as a blind person, myself, I am convinced that I could get a hit off of the best pitcher in the Major Leagues if you will allow me to change only one rule in baseball. Instead of three strikes, if you will give me an unlimited amount of strikes, I will persevere and endure until I inevitably get a hit.

Our lives are like a game of baseball with unlimited strikes. We're not counted out until we give up, throw down our bat, and walk away. The greatest opportunities come disguised as problems. The whole world is praying for a great idea, when all you and I need to do to have a great idea is simply to go through our daily routine, wait for something bad to happen, and then ask ourselves how we could have avoided that. The answer to that simple question will lead you to a great idea.

Furthermore, the only thing you need to do to have a great business is to ask yourself, "How can I help other people avoid that problem?" The universe will give you fame, fortune, success, and everything you ever wanted if you will simply help other people solve their problems. When you come to understand this reality, you will see

## FOREWORD

an opportunity beyond every problem and a victory just past every failure.

I hope you will enjoy this journey with Cheryl within this book. But more importantly, I hope you will allow her words to refocus your effort and energy so that you will enjoy the journey of your life. If so, I am convinced that the best is, indeed yet to come.

Jim Stovall
Best-selling author of *The Ultimate Gift*
www.JimStovall.com

## ABOUT THE AUTHOR . . .

Jim Stovall has been a national champion Olympic weightlifter, the President of the Emmy Award-winning Narrative Television Network, and a highly sought after author and platform speaker. He is the author of the best-selling book, *The Ultimate Gift*, which is now a major motion picture starring James Garner and Abigail Breslin.

Steve Forbes, President and CEO of Forbes magazine, says, "Jim Stovall is one of the most extraordinary men of our era."

For his work in making television accessible to our nation's 13 million blind and visually impaired people, The President's Committee on Equal Opportunity selected Jim Stovall as the Entrepreneur of the Year. He was also chosen as the International Humanitarian of the Year, joining Jimmy Carter, Nancy Reagan, and Mother Teresa as recipients of this honor.

# PREFACE

Failure—the other F-word we can't say.

Failure is a terminal word that often gets caught in people's throats—literally. We can't say it. We can't do it. We can't even think it. Why? This is what I call a judgment word—a word that gets a bad rap in my opinion. Judgment is a choice. WE give these words meaning.

What if you're wrong?

What would you do if you couldn't fail? EVER? What if failure was THEE single best thing that ever happened for you? What if failure was a gift? What if failure wasn't the end, but the beginning?

> *Success is not final; failure is not fatal.*
> *It is the courage to continue that counts.*
>
> —Winston Churchill

Failure has the perception of finality that few can think about. We take it personally. When we fail, we think it is permanent. When we get it wrong, we hear "we suck." We hear there is something wrong with us. We are unlovable, we are undeserving. We hear that WE are the

## FAILURE HAS NO ALIBI

failure. We take failure VERY personally. We let failure stop us.

I know because it stopped me . . . for more than 30 years.

Once we realize that there are no short cuts, there are no ways to hide, that failure has no alibi—-solutions will come, success will find us as it was always meant to be.

> *Success is where opportunity and preparedness meet.*
> —SENECA

Read on.

# CHAPTER 1
# THE FIRST F

High school is not something I would want to repeat ever . . . at any price. I am one of those annoying folks you knew in high school. You know the type, the brainiac, always had her nose in a book, always studying, always the one who raised the test curve. You know the type, salutatorian in junior high, en route to valedictorian in high school . . . etc etc etc.

However, senior year presented a challenge (saw that coming, right?). Calculus BC stood between me and my final A to attain that brass ring and join the ranks of the elite—the group of 10 of us that year in 1985 at Wheeling High School—all with perfect GPAs.

I remember the first day of this class like it was yesterday (and I can hardly remember what I had for breakfast!).

The beginning of my senior year in high school started with yet another Advanced Placement (AP) class to add to my college prep transcript. I walked into my last math class—Calculus BC—the advanced class for those bound for college. I met the teacher and on the chalkboard were all these hieroglyphics with this equation on the board.

### FAILURE HAS NO ALIBI

Mr. Smith welcomed us, introduced himself, and said, "When class is over, you will know how to solve the equation on the board!"

In my head I'm thinking, *What equation? There isn't one number on the board!???*

The whiteboard had integral signs and derivatives and other hieroglyphics. I had no idea what they meant. I was about to find out—to my chagrin and horror.

The first semester, I held my own. I struggled, barely earning my A, but earning, nonetheless. Thank goodness for partial credit as I was so worried about the hard stuff of Calculus that I often missed the simple stuff. The joke was that in my world, 2 + 2 = 5 (instead of 4!), always giving me horrendous answers because a simple arithmetic mistake impacted the final answer. Mr. Smith had exhaustible patience, always finding that nit noid arithmetic error; trying to reassure me that my calculus wasn't really the problem. My **confidence** was the problem. My fear of failure was the problem.

Then **THAT DAY** came.

I earned my first C.

I can **STILL** remember the pain I felt **to this day**.

Up to this point, I had never earned ANYTHING less than an A/ A- —EVER.

My first C was traumatic. I sat there simply stunned, fighting back tears in front of all my classmates, thinking. *What the he** just happened here?*

# THE FIRST F

Other students seemed to take these test grades in stride, reminding me that this wasn't the final grade for the class. This one test was just one of the many grades along the way.

Here is the interesting part of the story. Many people know the most important appliance in the house—the refrigerator. All rites of passage happened here: the first kindergarten drawing, the first handprint, the mother's day gift handmade of popsicle sticks for mom, pictures from the family vacation, birthday cards from grandma etc etc etc.

For some, their A's were trumpeted for all the world to see and celebrate. Some earned a buck an A! (I would have made a killing!).

Not me.

Getting A's for me was no big deal; nothing unusual, nothing new to see here.

UNTIL the day the first C came. THAT was the grade that went on the refrigerator and was celebrated. (I was devastated!). THIS was the milestone heralded far and wide.

Then the next milestone . . . yes—you saw this coming—my first F.

My **FIRST EVER F**. No it didn't stand for fantastic.

I can still see the paper, the **BIG BOLD RED F** staring back at me in the face, shocking everyone in the class, including me as I tried to hold back the tears. How could this happen? I was working harder than I had ever in my life and still I couldn't get it. It came so easy for some of the students. Several were simply geniuses. Several didn't have to study at all, they said. They even tried to explain it to me and talked until they were blue in the face. IT WAS HOPELESS. *I MUST REALLY SUCK*, I thought. I felt I was an idiot, because no matter what I did, I just didn't get it.

For the first time in my life, I truly felt stupid and hopeless.

That **F** made it to the front of the refrigerator door—holding court for many weeks as a reminder of my failure.

Every morning I saw as I had breakfast, mocking me, haunting me, taunting me.

I had nightmares being chased by integral signs in my dreams. I was holding on way too tight.

**Failure has no alibi.** There were no excuses. I simply wasn't good enough . . . yet.

There was only the need to dig even deeper, working the hardest ever in my life. The question was would it be good enough?

When the going gets tough, the tough get going.

There wasn't anything I couldn't master, right? (So the saying goes . . .)

I stayed after school for days on end. I worked with my teacher and my tutor—-determined to master this class if it killed me. **It nearly did.**

# THE FIRST F

If you focus on the learning, the grades will come. If you focus on the grades, the ulcers will come . . . And come they did, as did the migraines and the nightmares.

I couldn't help but wonder, "*Why was I doing this? Would it be worth it?*"

I was able to squeak by with my coveted A that term, but barely—-by the hair of my chinny chin chin! However, I was exhausted. I became sick.

No celebration. Simply a weak smile—as I remembered the pain of that F that mocked me on the refrigerator, an event that would haunt my dreams.

I know **now** what my parents were trying to do. They wanted me to understand that failure was simply part of the process of learning.

I didn't get it back then.

They didn't help me process this internally. I didn't know yet how to do on my own.

What I heard and felt, was "*I suck.*" "*I wasn't good enough.*" "*The F was me.*" "*I was the failure.*"

I failed in more ways than just earning the F on that test. My inability to process failure would remain my greatest legacy . . . there was no way out but forward.

**Failure has no alibi.**

\*sigh\*

It would be decades before I would truly understand.

# CHAPTER 2
# THE DAY THE MUSIC DIED

**University of Illinois-Champaign / Urbana.
Sophomore year. 1987.**

I remember that fateful day as if it happened yesterday. There was no warning. There was no preparation. My life forever changed in an instant.

I was a sophomore at the University of Illinois. I was the only undergrad in a graduate classical organ program in The School of Music. My professor was the renown Dr. Gerald Hamilton. If you wanted one person's opinion in this field of classical organ artistry—his was the one to get. He was talented, brilliant, a true artist, and one of the best classical organists in the business. I thought I had arrived to have the honor and privilege to study with HIM.

I had been playing since I was 5 years old. I was training to be a cathedral organist. Perhaps one day I would play the coveted pipe organ at Notre Dame in France, perhaps

**FAILURE HAS NO ALIBI**

Holy Name Cathedral in Chicago. I could only dream. I could only practice. I could only hope.

Failure wasn't an option.

I was Valedictorian at Wheeling High School. There wasn't anything I couldn't do.

**UNTIL** that fateful day, when the unthinkable happened.

My professor walked into my practice room and changed my life forever. He said I would not be allowed to take my jury to move on to be an upper classman.

*A **jury** is a final performance exam on your instrument for a musician, a confirmation one was ready to move to the next level.

I wasn't even allowed to try. My time at The School of Music was simply over. I should find a new line of work, he said.

He walked out.

    I heard the click of the door close behind him.

    My life was never the same.

This was the day the music died, as in the famous Don McLean song.

I remember sitting there on the organ bench with my *Orgelbüchlein* (Translation: Little Organ Book, a set of 45 chorale preludes for organ). I had my organ shoes on (specialized shoes in which to play the organ pedals). I sat there too stunned to move.

# THE FIRST F

What just happened? How could HE—in one defining moment—take away my dream?

I don't know. But he did. And he didn't break a sweat as he walked out.

I can't remember exactly how long I sat there trying to wrap my head around what had just happened. I was numb. I failed. I was dismissed. I was done. "Find another line of work," he said... indeed. I kept replaying those words over and over in a constant loop in my mind as in a bad horror movie. It was surreal.

**Failure has no alibi.**

There was no plan B.

There was no exit strategy.

This was the unthinkable.

Being dismissed from the program wasn't even a possibility I had considered, yet arrive it did without warning.

There was no petition. There was no appeal. One day, my career in music was just over.

In time, the tears came. The anger swept over me like a tidal wave. All I could think about were the tens of thousands of hours I had spent practicing since I was 5 years old, the sacrifices, the awards (didn't he know I won awards da*n it?!!@#$!).

What I failed to understand was that efforts are not outcomes. It didn't matter the time I put in; what mattered were the results. Could I play? Obviously, but not well enough.

Then the realization and panic hit.

*"Oh my God, what would I tell my parents?"*

I had quite literally *begged* them, *pleaded* with them to let me be a music major—to the chagrin of my father.

My dad would be right. I would never make it as an organist. He never wanted me to study music in the first place. Oh would he be vindicated!

The humiliation. The embarrassment. THE EPIC FAILURE!

What would I tell my friends?

What would I tell my family?

**What would I tell myself?**

In the end, what mattered most was what I told myself. The voice from high school surfaced again DECLARING IN ONE LOUD VOICE that I simply wasn't good enough . . . again. Period.

Dr. Hamilton only wanted the elite, the best of the best. I was not. I could not be part of the team. My career ended in 3 semesters. I wasn't allowed to try. I was found wanting.

While all of my friends in The School of Music were preparing for their juries, their next step in their careers to becoming an upper classman, I remember walking out

# THE FIRST F

of Smith Music Hall (where the organ practice rooms were) on the U. of I. campus one last time . . . never to return.

I collected my organ music, my red bag, and my organ shoes. I heard the click of the door behind me and I walked out of the hallowed halls of Smith Music Hall forever . . . tears streaming down my face, unable to make sense of it all.

There was no marching band, no clap of thunder, no one to hold my hand and tell me it was going to be ok . . . just a final click of the door shutting behind me. That was it. A piece of me died with my dream that day.

Music was dead to me. I wouldn't play again for more than 30 years.

# CHAPTER 3
# FAILURE CAME IN WAVES

In the days that followed, the voice of failure would come in waves, as a constant reminder at every turn that as the semester ended, others were moving forward, passing their juries with flying colors, earning their next step in the process.

For me, the world stopped spinning and came to a grinding halt.

I landed in my academic counselor's office trying to "find a new line of work." I transferred to the College of Liberal Arts and Sciences (LAS) and became a Music History Major with a Communication Minor. I would still salvage my college career at the University of Illinois. With taking summer school, I could still squeak by and graduate in the originally planned 4 years.

My diploma would look different. The path would be different, but I would still graduate with a bachelor's degree from the coveted Big 10 University of Illinois—but things didn't go as planned.

## FAILURE HAS NO ALIBI

In my mind, even with my diploma in my hand, **I failed**.

I was angry. I was hurt. I was shocked. I was alone. This failure didn't happen to anyone else I knew—just me.

What was missing was the ability to process failure. I took it personally. My professor gave me a gift, yet I did not recognize or receive as a gift at the time. Instead, I let it stop me. I heard, "I suck. I am not good enough. I failed."

I had a confidence problem. I became hesitant, cautious, timid, and fearful. I second guessed myself all the time. I cried . . . a lot.

What I needed was a mentor. I needed time to grieve. I needed time to heal. I needed time to process. I had none of the above.

I did what many typically do. I avoided. I was in denial. I turned my 1980s rock 'n' roll music WAY up REALLLLLLY LOUD to drown out the voices in my head. I shifted. I found a new line of work.

I endured the humiliation. I endured the embarrassment. I wore my failure as a scarlet letter. I let this failure define who I was. I became stuck. AND MOST IMPORTANTLY, I **stayed** stuck.

My response?

"If The School of Music doesn't want me, then I don't want them! If I wasn't good enough, then I wouldn't play at all, d*rn it! I would show them."

## FAILURE CAME IN WAVES

Sadly, the only person I showed was me and how weak I was. I showed the world what a coward I was as I accepted and internalized this failure. I decided I wouldn't play again. This failure was too painful. I stopped.

I didn't play for more than 30 years.

**I made the choice** to let the music die.

I could have done all kinds of things. I could have changed schools (But I had already changed schools once!). I could have simply continued to play at the local church on Sundays.

**Aside:** This is where I probably owe a few folks an apology. I was the lead foot who woke everyone up on Sunday mornings at St. John's Church in Champaign (*chuckle*). I just loved the power of the pipe organ. The energy, the sheer force, the POWER that I could summon at the mere touch of a button was nothing short of magical. It was incredible!!!! The earth moved under my feet . . . literally and figuratively. How could I possibly walk away from that which filled my soul?!!!!

Yet walk away I did from that holy instant, that defining moment.

I made the wrong choice.

Music became painful for me. What once was my safe place, my saving grace, my sanctuary, my church, became a place I could no longer go.

I couldn't process my love of music.

Being a music major is different than other majors in college.

**Music isn't what you *do*;
music is who *you are to your very core*.**

And I heard was I sucked. I heard I wasn't good enough. I internalized this message and took the lesson to my very core.

This wasn't just any F on the refrigerator. This was THEE F on the refrigerator door of life and I was found wanting yet again.

Goodbye dream of Notre Dame and Holy Name Cathedral. I had already said goodbye to the Marching Illini as Dr. Hamilton said I could be an organist, or I could be in the marching band. I could not do both. I chose classical organ.

A few semesters later, classical organ didn't choose me.

I walked away from the band as well. Music was simply too painful. All of my friends got their shot, many went on (and have since become!) amazing band directors and musicians and stayed in the business of music. I walked away, nearly running at breakneck speed from what had once consumed my heart and soul.

Herein lies an important aspect of this book. Failure has no alibi. There was no hiding in the shadows. There was no making excuses. There were no explanations. The answer was simple. The alibi was simple. I wasn't good enough. Move on. Period. End scene.

## FAILURE CAME IN WAVES

I should have sought out a mentor. I should have sought out a counselor. I could have made different choices. I could have seen the situation differently. I could have seen that failure would become my greatest gift, my most powerful ally, my greatest legacy.

I was too young. God gives you the skills and the talent way before one learns the maturity in which to wield these tools. Oh to be able to give my younger self advice, a loving hug, a lifeline, a mentor, a different way forward, a gift at such a young age. I could tell her it was going to be ok. I would be ok. I was good enough, always, and forever, just the way I was—imperfections and all.

I might have stayed in the business of music. I might have kept music as a hobby, played the occasional wedding or funeral, or just played for fun to fill my soul.

I did what many do when faced with conflict. They run. I ran as fast and as quickly as I could so I could stop the pain. I watched a dream die a slow and painful death. I found a new line of work.

In the decades that followed, I began to understand and unravel these mysteries of failure.

This was not my first failure. It would not be my last. Not even close.

The universe had way more to teach me . . . the question was whether I was ready to learn.

**I was not.**

# CHAPTER 4
# PART DEUX: LOST LOVE

This chapter is the most difficult for me to write, representing the greatest loss and failure of all . . . the loss of the loves of my life.

**A Tale of Two Cities**

It was the best of times; it was the worst of times . . .

The beginning phrase of this iconic book encapsulated my college career. Charles Dickens was a genius in describing the best and worst existing in the same moment.

I was the sickest I had ever been, yet life offered the sweetest happiness I had ever known. At one point, I had truly had it all and let it slip through my fingers like grains of sand through an hour glass.

Life shifted to open a new social world to me now that I had put my musical career behind me. I became a little sister at a fraternity, then eventually became a sorority girl myself. Who knew? It was never in the plan.

I met some of the most amazing people who became my college family. I remain friends with most of them to this day, more than three decades later. My advice? Choose your friends wisely during this important time in your life as they will shape and define the rest of your future.

I met the first love of my life toward the end of my sophomore year. I walked on a cloud. It was quite magical. It was a fairy tale. I simply lost myself in him like Cinderella at the ball. I couldn't believe I was that lucky. I wore his lavalier. I wore his fraternity pin. I did the candle lightings at my sorority. I became engaged—a heart shaped diamond adorned my finger the end of my junior year. What more could a girl want?

Then the unthinkable happened. He transferred to another college on the West Coast for our senior year. I was devastated. What could the universe possibly have in mind for such a cruel twist of fate?

This is where the story takes some interesting turns. My senior year was that tale of two cities of fame and legend by Dickens. It was one of the best years of my life, yet my fiancé played a very small role for most of it. I only saw him once each semester; once in the fall when he came for one of my major sorority events of the year (my crowning jewel as my sorority's social chair: Alpha Agents!). I went to his college for Spring Break (2 weeks!) in March. During the rest of the year, there were only weekly phone calls, as we moved further and further apart.

Because of being engaged to someone in the fraternity, I

## PART DEUX: LOST LOVE

found myself with a house full of older brothers to watch over me. I always had a date to their parties, campus events, or my sorority functions. I have never been so well taken care of in my life and so popular—every event often meant a different good looking fraternity guy on my arm. I was *so very* lucky. I had a ball that year if truth be told.

The dates were always meant to be platonic, simply an escort to a party as a big brother to take care of their fellow fraternity brother and his girl.

There was one relationship in particular that wasn't supposed to happen, but happen it did.

He was only supposed to be my date to parties like the others; someone to watch over me as a brotherhood thing while my fiancé attended his senior year. Then the unthinkable happened.

At first, he was simply a date, a flirty older brother. We always had a great time together. Then he became my ball room dance partner and the chemistry became unmistakable.

We kept things platonic. We tried very hard not to act on what we *thought* we felt. We kept coming up against what was expected of us, despite what chemistry told us was below the surface. We didn't sleep together. We never crossed that line. We stayed in the shadows as more than friends . . . no one knew how much more we both wanted . . . except us.

We may have fooled our friends, but we both knew there was something way more than either of us ever expected and we weren't prepared for it. We didn't have the maturity to help us know how to navigate these unchartered waters at such a young age. We didn't want to hurt anyone. Falling in love with another while I was engaged wasn't supposed to happen.

After graduation senior year, I gave the engagement ring back to my fiancé as I realized I was engaged to a man I simply didn't know any more. We changed dramatically that senior year while he was away; we simply didn't change together. We only saw each other once each semester. A year in college seemed like a life time in the real world. Our relationship just didn't make sense to me anymore. I couldn't quite separate my feelings. I had thought we might continue to date and get to know each other again once he returned. I didn't feel right in wearing his engagement ring with such uncertainty.

I didn't realize that when a girl gives an engagement ring back, it is over IN THAT MOMENT AND FOREVER. I never saw him again after that day. The memory still haunts me. I know that for him, I was the love of his life. For me, I wasn't sure.

Was I a horrible person for being honest? Was it arrogance and pride that ended the relationship because of potential feelings I had for another? I didn't know how to handle it all. I wasn't prepared. I couldn't tell anyone that I was torn between two men because the second one

## PART DEUX: LOST LOVE

wasn't supposed to happen. What a horrible person they would believe me to be if they knew what was in my heart. I was a coward and I couldn't tell them. I was a coward and couldn't tell my fiancé either. I walked away instead.

In the end, karma is a b*****. I ended up with neither of them.

I felt I was being punished for my failures yet again.

In 2011, my former fiancé took his life. He had been married twice, as had I. I couldn't help but wonder what might have been had I said yes instead of giving the ring back that fateful day simply because I was unsure of so many things back then.

Failure? I'll never know for sure what was really meant to be, but I always wonder what could have been. I know for sure that the choices I made broke his heart. There is no denying that. I haven't quite forgiven myself completely for how things happened. The way I broke his heart was the way my heart stayed broken as well. Perhaps I had planted the seeds of my own destruction because of my own arrogance and pride.

Life does level the playing field. The universe had so much left to teach me. Sadly, I left a few broken hearts in my wake as I began to learn about love and the many gifts it offered. College is a proving ground, a learning opportunity. Not all of us get it right to get the happy ending or the happily ever after.

After college, the other guy and I started dating. This is where karma reared its ugly head. When we could get together, the chemistry was definitely there. There was no doubt. In his words, we had epic times together; the memories still make me smile in ways most will never understand. Our feelings were intense. We could be in the same room and never say a word, yet there was an unmistakable connection. He could hold my hand and just smile, and I would quite literally melt. I would lose myself in his eyes in ways I never thought possible. He would serenade me, and I was in another world (Yes this man had amazing pipes!). He was so thoughtful and careful with me, and such a romantic as I had never known.

Our feelings scared the both of us I suspect as I know they scared me. I had never felt this way, not to the depth of my core. I knew this was more than just a fling. This wasn't simply lust (we never slept together, remember?) There was so much more that would take me years to unravel and understand.

I had it all—at one time. And I let him and us slip through my fingers as I was not strong enough to safe guard his heart or mine. The one person he should have been able to trust was me. And I don't know if he ever truly trusted me completely. He and I have both struggled with our personal lives over the years as a result. I can't help but think I'm responsible. I can't imagine what he must have felt; always feeling second best as when we first fell for each other, I wore another man's ring. Our love wasn't supposed to happen . . .

## PART DEUX: LOST LOVE

If only if I knew then what I know now.

The challenge was that he was in med school and I hardly saw him, and I couldn't wait. Patience remains a life lesson for me. If I could have only waited for him, I might have just had it all.

It wasn't his fault. It was mine.

He was a resident, 36+ hour shifts, odd hours, always seemingly on call, trying to make it in the program. He was immersed in his life as a doctor-to-be, **as he should have been.**

I was the impatient one. Had I met the man of my dreams? Could I get this lucky twice in a lifetime? Maybe. I simply wanted to spend time with him. Our chemistry was undeniable. He didn't have the time I needed and wanted; it wasn't his fault. We never said the I love you words, as we never knew for sure . . . but I always suspected.

With a love like that, I just wanted to see him, but fate seemingly stepped in.

I behaved like a heart sick teenager with her first crush who simply wanted his attention. When I couldn't get it, I sought the attention in the arms of another instead. I dated, eventually married, and moved on, assuming I could simply replace him, by substituting someone else for that hole in my heart.

Life would teach me that I couldn't . . . twice.

It took me years to figure out that I had given him my heart and there was no getting it back.

In my two failed marriages, I was never happy and never quite knew why or what was missing. I had failed. All of my friends who were married were happy and having families. They glowed with marital bliss. I wondered what was wrong with me as I didn't. I tried to be positive and find ways to enjoy the marriage experience. I couldn't. I often asked if there was something wrong with me. Was I simply one of those who was just never meant to be a wife or mother? Why wasn't I good enough to get the happily ever after? Maybe I should never have been married in the first place.

We told ourselves that we simply moved on (at least I did or tried to). The challenge for me is that I never did move on completely, at least not as far as my heart was concerned. It would take me years after my second divorce to make complete sense of it all. I didn't realize that I gave my heart away back then and for more than 30 years it has remained in his hands. I wondered if he even knew. I stayed away. I remained in the shadows.

The problem is that we never broke up officially. The feelings never stopped, at least for me. We simply walked away. I walked away. Sound familiar?

Just like my music that I put in a box and buried in the back of my closet for more than 30 years, this box found a companion to keep company with on that shelf. I found another box for him and placed that box right next to my failed music dreams.

## PART DEUX: LOST LOVE

Failure #2? Yes, most definitely.

I lost the greatest love of all and I didn't even know the depth to which it would haunt me for the rest of my life.

Time simply passed.

More than 30 years later, as I write this book the chemistry remains for me as does the longing for a love I never knew existed to this depth. Will we ever get that chance again? Will there be a part deux?

I have had to simply surrender it all to the universe. I don't know the answers as this part of the story is yet to be written. Time will tell whether fate may intervene yet again.

# CHAPTER 5
# FAILURE IS A GIFT

We make the best decisions we can with what we know at the time. A friend of mine told me that. He's right. We do not have to be happy about it. Simple. Not easy.

For someone who had not failed until their Senior second semester in high school, apparently I had a lot of catching up to do.

Perhaps it's true. The first F was the hardest. There were so many more to come. I had no idea that this was simply the beginning.

Charles Dickens had it so right. These were the best of times; they were the worst of times.

I had spent some of thee most amazing years of my life at U. of I.

My motto seemed to be—go big or go home. I had some of my most amazing successes and some of thee most epic failures nearly sequentially.

My life shifted my Junior year. I became a little sister

at the fraternity. I joined the sorority. I had many milestones that I achieved in college.

The highs were high; the lows were low. What I needed was to find balance and look at failure as simply a tool to help me process all that happened. Only in the decades that followed did I start to truly understand the lessons—the gifts—that Dr. Hamilton and the two loves of my life gave me that came from these failures.

Yes, Dr. Hamilton offered me a gift that fateful day. No I didn't see it that way at the time. What he offered me was another way forward. This was my first experience with forced compliance. If you wanted one person's opinion in the cut throat world of music, his was the one to get.

I do wish he would have been kinder in that moment. Perhaps he could have helped me process. Instead, in his matter of fact monotone way, he simply offered me the gift of reinvention, to take a new path.

He was right.

Yes, Dr. Hamilton. If you are reading this, wherever you are in the afterlife, know that I get it . . . now.

I tried decades later to look him up and thank him. I missed him by several years as he died before I got my act together and realized that what he gave me was a gift that was a defining moment for me.

Timing is not in my wheelhouse apparently.

## FAILURE IS A GIFT

**Failure has no alibi.** There is no sugar coating this. There is no explaining it away. There is no excuse that could make it right. There is only my need to be accountable for the part that I played in all of it, literally and figuratively.

Failure isn't supposed to be a long-term solution, but a short-term process along the way to *get to* success. One simply gets up one more time than one falls down. We learn. We process. We get up to fight another day. Except I didn't do any of this. I kept two of my biggest failures in their respective boxes in the back of my closet—-gifts that could have changed my life in those defining moments—had I been able to see them as gifts, instead of permanent failures. I chose to see failure as punishment for crimes committed by me.

Life happens for us, not to us. Perhaps life would still help me set things right.

## CHAPTER 6
# TURN INTO THE WAVE

Failure is what many fear and what many run from— as far and as fast as their legs can carry them. The solution is to fight our instinct to run away. Instead, we need to turn into the wind. Yes, you read that correctly, turn **into** the wind.

This action is counterintuitive. Firefighters and first responders are those specifically trained to run **into** a burning building or **into** disasters. I'm not suggesting that we go out of our way to seek disaster or intentionally place ourselves in harm's way if that is not our vocation. I am however suggesting that when conflict happens, when the unthinkable happens, we don't run away or hide.

I am someone who loves to kayak. If I had my way, I would be on the water all the time. I find water calming, peaceful, a way to shut off the voices in my head so that I can listen to my heart speak.

Despite my best efforts to get on the water before anyone else, I must share this piece of paradise with others, to include the speed boats and the jet skiers (and the occasional Seaplane in Seattle!). These devices cause a wake or waves. The bigger the boat, the faster the boat, the bigger the wake.

For someone in a kayak, the waves can potentially be a challenge, turning an otherwise calm and peaceful sport into a white water adventure. Unless you turn **into** the wave. Yes, **INTO**, not away from the wave. When I turn the nose of the kayak perpendicular **into** the wave, calmness resumes. Now I am working **with** the wave and Mother Nature, instead of against her. Simple physics. While the waves can get a bit bumpy, I am able to manage far more easily than if I choose to ride the wave to manage and mitigate its energy.

Here is the secret. We can **choose** to make a different choice. We can **choose** to turn into the wave. We can **choose** to turn into the wind. We can **choose** to turn into the conflict. We can fight the conflict head on, instead of running away.

Instead, many of us become reactive firefighters, choosing to react instead of leading ourselves forward from the conflict. I could simply allow the kayak to float aimlessly in response to the waves, really throwing someone like me with vertigo into a tailspin, particularly difficult on the water. OR I could **choose** to turn into the wave and ride it out, working with nature instead of against it. This strategy allows the return to stasis far more quickly.

The question to ask yourself is what are you fighting? (Often ourselves!) Stop. Take a breath. Turn your kayak into the wind. Face the conflict. Process the failure. Take control. Lead yourself.

# TURN INTO THE WAVE

**Make another choice.**

The solution is that to go faster, we must slow down. We must take the time NOT to go around obstacles and avoid conflict. We must stand our ground and face the music (pun intended) and move forward.

In the kayak, I could choose to ride the bumpy waves and hang on for a bumpy ride allowing Mother Nature to toss me around until the energy in the wave subsides OR I could try to paddle quickly out of the direction of the waves. However, unless you have some serious muscles and quick reaction time on a small lake, there often isn't time. I could take the long way around and hug the shore line to get back to the safety of the kayak launch as well. OR I could simply and purposefully turn **into** the wave, and take the shortest path forward, which is a straight line. Purposeful. Intentional. Difficult. Painful.

Reaction is a choice. Choosing to do nothing is a choice. Choosing the bumpy path is a choice.

**Failure has no alibi.**

Choosing the straight path through the conflict quickly is a choice. There are no short cuts. We must do the work. The more we avoid, the more we go around, the more we delay, the longer the process will take.

The universe will give you the lesson over and over again like groundhog day. How many of the same days do you want to live through? Be strong. Choose wisely. Remember, **failure has no alibi.**

# CHAPTER 7
# CHOOSE TO DANCE

Consider this question. Is failure a predator to fear or a dance partner to follow? The choice is ours. We all react to failure differently. The initial response is similar—that moment of fight or flight is the holy instant of how we respond. Do we slay the dragon as something to protect ourselves against at all costs as I did? Do we panic? Do we take flight as fast as our legs will carry us? Do we simply take it all in, calmly, coolly, as a matter of course?

Our natural response is to avoid fear at all costs. We would not put ourselves intentionally in a position to be hurt. This is why so many people stay single, isn't it? Love can be the most amazing experience of your life or the most painful nightmare to endure. Why? Like failure, love is a feeling. And fear is nothing more than an acronym: False Evidence Appearing Real. We choose to react to feelings. We choose to believe even in the absence of evidence.

> *Evidence of absence is not the same as the absence of evidence.*
> —Martin Rees

Read this statement again slowly. Listen deeply.

Pain is not necessarily a bad thing, particularly from a medical standpoint. Those who cannot feel pain suffer from a condition known as congenital insensitivity to pain (CIP). This condition (also known as congenital analgesia), is a rare conditions in which a person cannot feel (and has never felt) physical pain. Pain is intended as a warning sign, a beacon of hope to perhaps stop before things really hit the fan, to stop doing something that is wrong or hurtful or to get help from others because you can't go it alone. Hint: Life isn't supposed to be a solo event. Contrary to what many might tell you, **you can't dance by yourself.** (Even line dancing is a group event!).

Couple dancing by definition is with a partner. The universe uses balance here—the yin and yang, the ebb and flow, black and white, the negative and the positive. Nature has had these answers from the creation of the universe. Mother Nature knows.

**Failure can be an amazing teacher
IF WE CHOOSE TO FOLLOW her lead.**

We can learn its lessons. We can heed its warning. We can be in gratitude with its blessings.

With women, the dance metaphor is a bit tricky as in the traditional male / female partnership, women can **only** follow. IF you have a weak leader as your partner, you may look awful on the dance floor. If they give you the wrong cue, if they step on your feet, you're sunk. As a woman, your dance partner can be your greatest asset or your most challenging liability. Our partner can make us look amazing, sometimes even better than our talent skill may suggest or as if you have never danced a step.

The secret is to be in concert with your partner. They cannot lead if you will not follow. This is leadership by definition, where it quite literally takes two to tango. The converse is also true. If you will not follow, they cannot lead. Failure is a teacher who stays until the lesson is learned (like ground hog day!). Once learned, the student moves on to the next lesson. If not, the lesson repeats and repeats and repeats.

The question to ask yourself is how long do you want to spend on this same lesson?

The faster you learn, the faster you move on. **Fail faster, succeed sooner.** Facing failure head on is the fastest path forward.

Like dancing, failure takes practice. Remember my first F? The first F in high school was amazingly difficult. I didn't know what I didn't know. I had to really step up my game. With hard work, tenacity, perhaps true grit, and downright stubbornness, I was able to master what I needed to gain my desired outcome.

I was on the right track to understanding failure, but then I took the coward's way out. My two biggest failures—the day the music died and losing the loves of my

## FAILURE HAS NO ALIBI

life—I was a coward. The pain was just too much to face alone. I didn't have the right people in my life to help me process, so I ran. I put both into a box, slammed the lid shut, and ran like a bat out of h*ll. I thought I could hide forever and simply pretend these boxes didn't exist.

Remember, **failure has no alibi.** You can run, but you can't hide. If we tire of the pain, if we can find the strength, the universe finds a way to bring your life full circle.

**When the student is ready, the teacher will come.**

The messenger for me was music. It seemed only fitting that the messenger would come back using music since this was the gift I tried so hard to keep in that box. As I healed other areas of my life, the universe offered an opportunity for reflection. I once more said yes.

The chapter on love remains in progress. To break a curse, is to trust love. Ultimately, we must trust ourselves. We must forgive ourselves for the sins of our past. It is hard to trust love again when you couldn't the first time. Again, a willing partner is needed. Marriage is indeed intended as the ultimate partnership to ensure that one goes through life leaning against another so that neither falls down. I don't want the man I can live with; I want the man I can't live without . . . a seed planted in the days of my collegiate youth.

I now recognize failure as the ultimate gift and teacher. Do I like it? Honestly? Not always. Even when we know

## CHOOSE TO DANCE

that pain is necessary, we don't have to like it. Although I do have a friend who suggests that if you can't beat 'em, join 'em; embrace the suck (Thank you Elizabeth!). If what we resist, persists, stop resisting. The harder the lesson, often the more painful the process, but the sweeter the pain. Life is quite the paradox, isn't it?

That which we avoid the hardest is that which we need the most.

What will you choose?

# CHAPTER 8
# ASK THE RIGHT QUESTIONS

The body knows. The heart knows. The body has always known the right answer. But I didn't know how to find these answers.

> **When we ask the right questions, the right answers will come.**

I wasn't asking the right questions. I wasn't looking in the right places. For some parts of my life, I simply stop looking altogether.

I have spent thousands and thousands of dollars trying to figure out the reasons for my health challenges. From the Mayo Clinic to the psychology couch to functional medicine, each promised that they had the answer, only to come up empty time and time again.

Just like Dorothy in the Wizard of Oz with her infamous ruby slippers, her journey taught her that she already had the answers she sought. She already had the power. There was nothing she needed. She was already whole, complete, healthy, and she had all the answers she would ever need. Her body knew. Her heart knew. Her friends knew. She told everyone she met—she was going home.

Who she had not yet convinced was herself. She lacked confidence. She lacked trust and faith in herself. She lacked the ability to see herself as the world saw her. She was and had always been good enough just as she was. She lacked for nothing.

I have always been good enough. I was always healthy and perfect as I was created. I simply didn't believe. From the first F to being dismissed from the classical organ program at the University of Illinois, from losing the loves of my life, I doubted the one person I should have been able to trust without question . . . me.

Others loved me just as I was! I didn't believe them because the body appeared broken. Fix the mind, listen to the heart, and the body follows.

I have been traveling my own yellow brick road, my own personal journey of self-discovery, only in my 50s did I discover that I didn't need others to love me to be good enough. I just needed me to love me. I was always complete, whole, and amazing—just as I am.

I didn't need others to make me happy. I could make myself happy. I didn't need to look outward to find happiness, to find love, to find inner peace and joy, to find contentment, to find fulfillment and success. I had always had all of these things all along—my own ruby slippers.

When you get your mind right, the body will follow. When you get your mind right, the heart will follow. If you follow your heart, you will never be lost.

**Failure has no alibi.**

Where does that energy go? The negative energy from our epic failures deposit in our mind and in our bodies. It impacts our wiring connections. It impacts how we show up in the world, who we love, and how.

I have always had the ruby slippers—both literally and figuratively. I have always had the power. I have always had the answers. I simply didn't ask the right questions. I didn't have the confidence to believe.

The secret is that to go faster, I needed to slow down. To find the love that I craved, I had to love me first. Instead of going in search of the answers in the outward world, all I had to do is go inward. I always had all that which I needed.

The body knows. The heart knows. I have always known. Now, as my body heals, the energy dissipates, the blockages clear, the energies transform from pain to joy.

I have become an athlete for the first time in my life. I could hardly walk and found myself in a wheelchair for 9 months less than 5 years ago. Now I can mountain bike up to 3 miles a day. I kayak 3–4 times a week. I take my Siberian Husky Gracie for a walk nearly every day.

I believe in me.

## FAILURE HAS NO ALIBI

The brain is a muscle we need to tap into. We must have faith first, *then* action follows. Most of us must **see** first, *then* we believe. We must instead take a leap of faith, then confirmation will come our way.

There is no place like home. Home is where we hang our hat. Home is where our heart is.

I have been running for years in search of the place I never want to leave. What I learned is that the home I was looking for wasn't a physical house; it wasn't a physical place; it wasn't a specific person. What I was searching for was learning to love me in all my brokenness **first**. If I didn't love me, why would anyone else?

Only when we accept and love ourselves as the Wicked Witch, can we find the beautiful Cinderella inside. She's always been there. We've always had the power to transform. We have always had the power to emerge from the shadows to reclaim our power and our rightful place and purpose in the universe. No one can do this for us. When we get it right, the world will unlock its many secrets to let us know that we are home. We have always been home. We simply have to trust the person we are inside to lead ourselves to where we have always wanted to go.

There is no place like home because we have never left. We have been home the whole time.

## CHAPTER 9
# WHAT IS YOUR LEGACY?

As a college professor, I use an exercise with my leadership students to have them write their obituary. If they were to die tomorrow, what would their obituary say on their behalf? The point of this exercise is in goal setting, putting the student in control as the captain of their ship where life happens *for* us, not *to* us. If we don't like what is, we have the power to change it—to rewrite the ending as our new future.

For those who have trouble with writing their obituary and the finality of the death conundrum, the alternative exercise is the ability to write their acceptance speech for receiving a humanitarian award.

I recall completing this exercise in my undergraduate years, then again at the master's level in graduate school, and then a final time at the doctorate level. During my undergraduate years, I was disappointed as I had little to write as I had not done anything quite yet. At my teacher's urging, I rewrote the ending in what I wanted my legacy to be as opposed to what it was staring back at me in black and white on the page. The purpose of the exercise is to realize that we have the control to rewrite the ending and find a new way forward instead of settling. By rewriting the ending, we can rewrite and predict a new future.

Many of my students find power in this exercise. We can take our control back in our lives to write our new story, to write our legacy that we **choose** to leave behind.

I have copies of my 10 year plans of all these amazing things I wanted to accomplish on my bucket list. I didn't get much of it right. I didn't stay married. I didn't (couldn't) have children. I didn't get the happily ever after ending—(at least not yet, but I still believe in love and remain a hopeful romantic!). The future of my legacy remains a path for which I have control.

Had it not been for Dr. Hamilton and dismissing me from the program, I would not have had the career that I have had thus far. I would not have been a professor (now 20+ years!). I would not have completed my master's and doctorate degrees. I would not have become a military wife of 23 years and traveled the world, moving 38 times. I would not have created a 25 time award winning publishing company with now 3 imprints, nor might I have published 45 books (and counting!) or helped mentor more than 77 doctoral graduates and earn more awards on the wall than I can count.

I have been very blessed in a career I never envisioned because I was forced in a new direction more in line with my talents and my gifts that I could be of contribution to the world.

## WHAT IS YOUR LEGACY?

My legacy also includes the teachings of Napoleon Hill and the inspiration he left behind as a result of the powerful insights from his life's journey. Napoleon Hill believed that what you think, you become. Control your thoughts, you control your destiny. In his various writings, *Law of Success* (1928), and *Think and Grow Rich* (1937), he offered 17 principles that when followed can lead to great success and personal achievement. These merit repeating again here.

## NAPOLEON HILL'S 17 PRINCIPLES OF SUCCESS

1. Definiteness of Purpose
2. Mastermind Alliance
3. Applied Faith
4. Going the Extra Mile
5. Pleasing Personality
6. Personal Initiative
7. Positive Mental Attitude
8. Enthusiasm
9. Self-Discipline
10. Accurate Thinking
11. Controlled Attention
12. Teamwork
13. Adversity and Defeat
14. Creative Vision
15. Health
16. Budgeting Time and Money
17. Habits

Thank you Napoleon for your willingness to share with us the lessons from your life's journey. Simple. Not easy.

# CHAPTER 10
# SPEAK FROM THE HEART

Speaking from the heart is when we have faith in who we are and speak from our core of what we believe, with no excuses and no qualifications, just what we believe from a place of love and kindness—the good, the bad, and perhaps even the ugly. No judgment, no agenda, no anger; it is what it is in all its truth and honesty.

We have the courage to be who we are without thought to qualification of what others think of us. Love us the way we are, for who we are, or walk away. We are enough that who we are right now. We don't need your approval. We stand before you imperfect but ok. We lack nothing. We ask for nothing. We live in service of love.

Wearing our heart on our sleeve is the victim mentality; the staying stuck because it is easier to make excuses. It is easier to blame others. It is easier to shrink and only say what is popular for which we find comfort in conformity and victimhood. We lack accountability. We are drama. We are tears. We are shame. We choose all of these because we lack the will to change because it will be hard, and we choose not to follow that arduous path.

## FAILURE HAS NO ALIBI

We embody the *woe is me attitude*, hoping others will share sympathy for our plight and our choices and feel sorry for us because that confirms we do not have to change.

Remember, **failure has no alibi!**

Life is choice. We can choose to do the hard stuff and look inward to share with others who we are. We risk you walking away. To know when we have arrived is to know that we no longer crave your acceptance because we have already accepted ourselves and have found ourselves to be enough—in all of our imperfectness.

This is no easy task.

I am the accomplished professor, 45 books, 25 awards, yet divorced not once, but twice. I believed what the world said back in high school and in college. I wasn't good enough. I sought the awards as external validation that despite my medical issues, my failed marriages, my lack of being able to have children, that I was ok—the awards said so.

That wasn't it. What I was looking for I could never find because the world cannot give me what I am searching for—-acceptance of me by me. For that, I am a work in progress.

Some days are better than others. Yes, even as externally accomplished as you see, I remain on a path learning to accept the worthiness of me. Am I there completely? No—not yet, but closer today than yesterday.

## SPEAK FROM THE HEART

It's raw. It's a risk. It's dangerous. So why am I responding this way? I'm willing to share in the most vulnerable way possible. Let me tell you that it is not easy. If I can do it, you can do it. Simply take a big leap of faith.

Ok—now is the hard part . . . to wait to see your reaction and whether this was what you were looking for and whether this may change our relationship going forward in some way. I hope so. Connection can be powerful IF we are willing to take such a risk.

## CHAPTER 11
## NO REGRETS

Timing is everything isn't it? No more than in 2020 having had our world turned upside down and inside out. Yet, the point is that we're still standing.

The dance metaphor is an important one to find perspective. When do we need to stay on the dance floor? When do we need to take a step back and go up to the balcony to see the big picture? When do we need to take others with us to the balcony? When do we lead, when do we follow? When do we simply get out of our own way?

When we are on the dance floor with our partner or partners (line dancing!), we can but see the immediacy of what is in front of us and perhaps directly around us.

We can lose perspective if we're not careful.

Let yourself dance. Give yourself permission to fly and dream. Despite the events of 2020, despite failures of the past or present, time is of the essence. There is no time to waste. We need to make peace with our past, to plan our present so as to preserve our future. Should the end come sooner than we imagine, will we be ready? No one ever died wishing they had worked more. Everyone always regrets what they didn't do. I want no regrets. I will celebrate my failures, even celebrate with Shakespeare that it is better to have loved and lost than never to have loved at all. I do not regret having become a musician. I regret wasting time to discover the gifts that while not good enough to perhaps play at the level of Notre Dame, I was plenty good enough for me. While I may not have married either of the loves of my life, I was blessed in meeting them and joining them on their journeys even if for only a short while. I knew once what it meant to be truly loved for me before I became who I am before you today.

Do we celebrate these lessons here? Yes. We must learn to forgive ourselves for who we were when we didn't know what we know now. How I wish I could have that conversation with my younger self at key cross roads in my life to love myself a bit more, to thump myself on the back of the head with a Cher moment of "Snap out of it!" or perhaps a Gibbs style head slap from NCIS.

No I didn't get it right during high school or college. I do have some amazing memories, epic tails, and fantastic stories of failure. Go big or go home. My final message is to help you live life to the fullest as in my motto from my sorority—Alpha Sigma Alpha. We have but one life to live, we shall but pass this way but once. For those I loved and lost, I am glad that we met. I am truly sorry I screwed it up; thank you for being part of my journey. I hope that you can look back fondly on the time we spent together and love me a bit more in those moments when I fell short of the mark. To realize our humanity is to realize we are not perfect. As much as we try to be, perfection is not realistic nor attainable. We will always fall short.

My wish for you is to keep showing up. Keep loving those around you, particularly more in those moments that we discover we are human and failed to meet the expectations of others. We simply have to keep getting back up one more time than we got knocked down.

Remember **failure has no alibi.** Own it. Be accountable for it. Love yourself a bit more because of it. Smile. Breathe. Know you deserve everything life has to offer. Ask. Your heart knows. Your heart always knows. Silence the voices in your head and let your heart speak. Have the courage to take the first step. You can have everything you want and more. Believe in yourself.

Know that I'm here. Know that I'm still standing. Know that life isn't over until it's over. We can still get up tomorrow to strive to be better than we were today. You've got this.

# ABOUT THE AUTHOR

Dr. Cheryl A. Lentz, affectionately known as *Doc C* to her students, is a university professor on faculty with Embry-Riddle University, Grand Canyon University (GCU), Capella University, and Walden University. Dr. Cheryl serves as a dissertation mentor / chair and committee member. She is also a dissertation coach, offering expertise as a professional editor for graduate thesis and doctoral dissertations, as well as faculty journal publications and books.

Awards include Walden Faculty of the Year, DBA Program, 2016, UOP community service award, USO Bronze Mission Award 2020, and 25 writing awards.

Dr. Cheryl is also an active member of Alpha Sigma Alpha Sorority.

Known as the Academic Entrepreneur, Dr. Cheryl is a unique and dynamic speaker who intensely connects with her audience, having one foot in academia and one foot in the business and entrepreneurial space. Her goal is to offer the audience pearls of wisdom today they can use tomorrow in their personal and professional lives. It is not enough to know; the expectation is for participants to take action and do. Join Dr. Cheryl on her journey to connect these dots to provide inspiration, knowledge, and counsel to move forward effectively.

Known globally for her writings on leadership and failure, as well as critical and refractive thinking she has been published more than 45 times. As an accomplished university professor, speaker, and consultant, she is an international best-selling author, and top quoted publishing professional on ABC, CBS, NBC, and Fox. She takes the stage as a TEDx Speaker in *Farmingdale2020, October 10, 2020.

To reach **Dr. Cheryl Lentz** for information on refractive thinking, professional editing, consulting or guest speaking, please visit her **website:** http://www.DrCherylLentz.com or **e-mail:** drcheryllentz@gmail.com

www.ingramcontent.com/pod-product-compliance
Lightning Source LLC
LaVergne TN
LVHW051850080426
835512LV00018B/3169